MERCURY EXPERIMENT

MERCURY MUSINGS

2014 / 2015

PREFACE

The Mercury Experiment was established in July 2013, and apart from the occasional guest sitters, it's just been Liz and myself who sit each week in her fully blacked-out, converted garage. The original idea was to set the room up and sit in the same way as the Scole Experiment Group, which developed impressive evidential physical phenomena and communications during the 1990s. *(Foy R.P. 'Witnessing the Impossible' Forcal Publications, 2008 - 2011)*

We started off sitting round a table with a glass dome in the centre and a quartz crystal and three ping-pong balls around it. We also had a separate monthly sitting, with Liz in the cabinet, and no table. More recently we've combined the two approaches, with Liz in the cabinet, and me sitting opposite her, with the table in the middle. We will probably modify things further in the future as the experiment evolves.

After the opening prayer, we start each session with a short visualisation, referred to as 'The Rainbow Bridge', following the protocol of the Scole Group. We then tell each other what we've experienced. Often our experiences are very similar, suggesting we've perceived the same thing, but interpreted it in our own way. We then continue with the session.

We have both experienced minor phenomena including changes in temperature, light touches and pulling feelings. We see changes in the atmosphere as it appears to become lighter or changes colour, and we also experience pin-pricks of light, streaks of light, patterns and flashes, and left or right side predominance.

Liz picks up words, including names, and images while she sits, and verbalises these as she gets them. This book contains extracts from what she has said during 2014 and 2015.

The full transcripts of the sittings may be accessed at *http://themercuryexperiment.blogspot.co.uk/*

Nick Pettitt,

March, 2016

INTRODUCTION

At first view, these transcripts may read like the crazy, jumbled, poetic ramblings of the subconscious mind, the superconscious mind, and the universal consciousness, all rolled into one. The peculiar flavour and aroma is mine.

The words recorded in these sessions represent, from one point of view, a mixture of mental noise, clairvoyant perceptions, precognitive flashes, inspirational visions, and, just possibly, some genuine attempts at communication from the dead. From another point of view, this communication may be conceived as part of a clairvoyant scanning of an extended consciousness information matrix, which includes memories and information of the dead. It is difficult to determine what it is. However, at the very least, these recordings yield some evidence of consciousness functioning independently of the normal physical restraints of time and space, and therefore independently of the physical body. And this is what has been requested, each session, in our opening prayer.

In support of this, three such instances could be highlighted. The first two suggest possible communcation from the dead. The third suggests precognitive clairvoyance.

In the first instance, a friend, Sheila, who was herself a medium, communicated details of her dying and death, after she had died, but before this fact was known to the participants. The fact of her death and these specific details of her dying were later confirmed by an independent and previously unknown party, who was relieved to know that Sheila was now at peace and very happy, as she had been disturbed by some of the experiences during her dying. *(see 03.02.2015)*

In the second instance, information was communicated concerning a little girl, who was perceived clairvoyantly. *(see full transcript at http://themercuryexperiment.blogspot.co.uk/ 12/05/2015)* The information caused me to contact a woman whom I had not seen for over fifty years. The communication proved very meaningful to her, as her young daughter had died some years before, (information unknown to Nick and myself), and the information received seemed relevant in many ways. Six months before this seance communication, my husband had had a lucid dream, in which a little girl appeared and told him her name, which was very unusual. In the morning he had asked me if I knew the meaning of this name, or anyone bearing it. I did not. I had looked the name up in a dictionary at the time. Six months later, after a little girl appeared in a seance, and after I had made contact with her mother, I discovered that the name of the dead child was the same as the name given by the little girl in my husband's lucid dream. It was confirmed that the age was similar, and that the hair colour was similar, and when her mother sent me a photograph, my husband recognised it as the girl in his dreams. My husband has never participated in these seances, or shown much interest, so this was an unusual linking of two independent evidential communications, separated by many months, and some space. The family was unknown to my husband, and the birth and death of the child were unknown to me, as my aquaintance with the family had been very brief, and fifty years ago. However, interestingly, my husband had a strong spatial and temporal connection with the context in which the family had been living for many years, and also the place where the child's ashes were scattered. The two independent pieces of evidence seem more than just coincidence, as the specific name of the child was very unusual in our culture and country.

The third instance involves possible precognition. During a seance, (see *http://themercuryexperiment.blogspot.co.uk/ 12.05.2015*) I found myself in Charleston Farmhouse, the country setting of the Bloomsbury set, looking at the wallpaper and hand decorations, and paintings, and considering the whole scene and ethos, and commenting on it, involving the literary community and their values. There also seemed to be a connection with the railway, which was mentioned. I had only been there once before, many years ago, and wondered why it had suddenly come into my consciousness with such vividness and clairvoyant transparency, as if I was actually there. Several days later, my son came to visit us in Sussex, travelling by train from Manchester. On arrival, he asked whether we might make a trip to Charleston Farmhouse. Apparently this was a sudden desire of his, as while on the train, he found himself reading an article about Charleston Farmhouse and the Bloomsbury set, and felt a strong impulse to visit the setting. We made the visit, and spent a pleasant Sunday afternoon at Charleston Farmhouse. I confirmed with him that he had not thought of Charleston Farmhouse until several days after the seance, while on the train journey to Sussex. As the thought had not entered his head until after the seance, and there had been no communication between us concerning the seance, and he has never attended or shown any interest in the seances, it seems possible that my consciousness was accessing and scanning a larger arena than the one understood by our normal linear view of time, ie it was seeing the future. Of course this could also be coincidence. However, perhaps the two explanations are not incompatible.

I know that these examples are meagre compared with some of the strong evidential communications and phenomena mediated by certain well-known and established mediums. However at the very least, they do seem to represent a response to our request for 'evidence of existence of consciousness independent of the physical body, and survival of consciousness beyond death.' I am grateful for these offerings. I hope that as we persevere in our experimental sittings, more evidence will surface, and become stronger, clearer, and irrefutable. And I hope that I will become a finer and more receptive instrument, capable of accurately relaying this evidence.

It seems that the nature of the evidence that we anticipate, consciously or unconsciously, may be very different from what is actually given and received.

Liz

March, 2016

Liz in the cabinet.

11/12/2013

In the final debacle the wizard is a person; but it's not a question of being cheated because the journey to the realization, a full humanity, is a parable. The scarecrow, lion and tin man become real and Dorothy finds her way home. So although it seems as if the wizard was a sham, the wizard was merely a device, a learning device, to encourage them to explore… That's okay. The wind is the important thing. Wind is the spirit that carries and starts Dorothy off on this journey

Keep coming back to the firebird and the question ' what's real in all this?' and the answer comes… 'underlying thread'. All the glittering appearances and the phenomena, all the great creative surge, all burnt in the fire. Experience and those ashes, that's the common thread, the ashes and the earth. But not to get too attached to all phenomena, the golden carriages, the incredible creativity, the ballets with performances, the charades, wonderful and magnificent but ultimately the common thread is the earth, the ash. Come back to basics, what's real in all this, a wonderful play, but not to get too caught up in it or get lost. Keep the thread, the common thread, the ash and delight in the flames, all pictures and shapes… You could keep wanting to come back for more, more shapes, more images, adventure…

30/01/2014

Steadfast, steadfast… like a ship going forward, it's got a cross… it's to do with the journey, keeping the direction, keep going forward, steadfast, a cross at the helm, it's the guiding connection, it's a direction… Must be with the right relationship with the earth, got to get the compass right, got to set the course and keep to it, not flinching.

Like a cloud, it's the warning, the locusts, plague, in a field, corn stalks, it's all dry, the crunch is the locusts, but it's to do with change, it's to keep to the old way of being in tune with the earth, just hold fast, there's a rocky time ahead, feel the beginnings of it now, but this boat, ship, keeps steadfast, keeps going forward but it's in touch with the old explorers, starship earth, just keep at the helm, set the course, set it according to the stars, according to the bones and the amethyst, it's a direction, just keep on, keep the faith

03/04/2014

The mountains, they're brilliant. Brilliant blue sky and the colours are radiant. The lambs become little goats, but it's a place where the spirits are air, the spirits are abundant but ever fine, the chiming of bells, this is a chorus. It is the temple of the sky

The sky is a brilliant deepest blue going to purple but I think the call is to bring all these spirits that have been working through illness, through all the conflicts of the worldly historical… bring them up to the top of the mountain, to the temple'

Not the temple of sacrificing the lambs, it's where the lambs will be fed. This is the place for the feeding of the lambs. The grass is rich and green and there are rainbows in the sky'

It's a great emptying of self, a purification. It's like going into a wonderful pool of crystal water... Union... That's the difference between the union, of the trade union, that was a shadow, wrought with conflict and struggle but the ideal is the union united. This is the union of spirit

Rise up, rise up on the internal, into the inner temple not the outer. Those are shadows, it's a shadow world. Those are the battle grounds, the testing of the spirit but then on the inner plane there has to be the purification... so let go of the conflict

Union, the new union, union of spirit. Beyond... this great emptiness of self and the crystal clarity of the sea which is to see and to be seen. It's all seeing in the sea, vision, light, it's the union of spirit, the union, the only trade is love... Feed my sheep. This means revealing the spiritual truth

22/05/2014

Community, comes from sharing, a sense of being united, enjoying shared endeavour and it's that that we need to get back. The simplicity and joy of a shared life, like bees, it's a harmony, to join in community, it's a blessing. Has the same effect as singing in a choir where everyone has their part but the whole comes together as a harmonious enterprise, created unison'

'It's the kaleidoscope, the pattern. Then you get bored, then it wears thin, with just a little wiggle and you change it. The same elements but a new look, a new way of seeing, a new pattern. And in community you come together, first one way in a joint enterprise, sharing and the elements break up and reunite and another way for another activity, like clouds... It's the same units but the union. The knack is the point of change, to let go of the pattern so a new one can start to form, so trust... It's like the bird has to break the shell to hatch. You have to let go of the old patterns and swim free from it and then the calling together, reconvening for new work is creation.

*This is the creation of new ways of being. Out of so many simple units repeated pattern you can get so many new formations...'
'Just a twist of the wrist and the pattern's broken and a new one begins to come into being, yeh, crystallization... But it has to melt, the crystals have to break up or it would just, everything would come to a standstill, frozen into immobility. But that's not the way, movement and change, reshaping like the clouds in the sky...'*

The great value of community, of the joint enterprise, of the sharing, of the striving together, to create and this is love in action. It's the expression, the true community... But from where I am now I can see the great value, the importance, joy... and these little enterprises like the kibbutzim, unions, all these social enterprises are a forerunner, a shadow, an expression, an attempt to create the love in action... enjoy, appreciate...

Shadow dancing, like on the sheet where you make the pattern and that's what the spirits are doing behind the scenes they're these efforts to reshape communities to come together all these enterprises where communities join they're inspired, they're the shadow dancing, we are breathing into them, we are the motivators, we motivate, so when you see these efforts to combine, to produce new communities, new ways of coming together you know that the motivation is from spirit... We're close behind; they're shadows of our love...

There are these invisible threads, runners, links, joining all these efforts together, into a mosaic, into a pattern. Then with one shake reforms and regroups it's all manifestation of our motivation of our thought...

To allow the shining to come through, to turn to the light, to remain a conduit, to feel part of this larger community, to be aware, being a nexus, a link, a hub... For the power to accumulate for these patterns, to reform, to reshape, to regenerate these links are necessary, focuses of the light, the power. This is what we're doing.

It's like we're the shadow dancers for the motivation for the spirit. For it to come through you need the conduit, the nexus, the hub, the focus and that provides the energy to shake the strings and the threads in the material world and along those threads the changes, the pattern can begin to jiggle and change. The energy can accumulate to affect that switch over. This is happening, pattern is changing but the energy to make that flip over, we need these hubs, these vortices, nexus, power centre and a force will travel along the threads out to give energy, to reshape and the time is coming when these new communities will form based on love, shared endeavour, all in the light, all united in love, in simplicity… in contentment…

04/09/2014

We're suddenly all being rolled up in a carpet; this journey is not quantifiable, it's not linear, it's not, when you try to get a sense of time scale it's all happening simultaneously at a higher level, a different perspective. You see the beginning and the end point, they're already there, all held not only in our perspective but on the low hills walking towards in a linear fashion, all times, old time, out of time, we can't quantify it here

The orange robes - they're transmitting, they have a lot of influence… The orange robes and black caps… Its old knowledge, old wisdom and they don't want it to be lost… crumbling, it's crumbling… a silence of sound

Sacred sacrament… It's to hold all things sacred; it's a very sacrilegious age… very, holding things sacred, that's the importance, the holding, the sacrament… That simple sacrament of bread and wine and the transmutation, it's a flash in the pan, some of the simplest everyday items become transformed to the sacred…'

'Testing to see if the lineage has survived…'

'It's a question of the key…'

a treasure chest full of sacramental objects. we're being asked to unlock it but its inside us, we've got the key,

to worship the sacred in the everyday, to value, to seek, to look into this treasure trove of the everyday ordinariness … that's the true worship

11/11/2014

In a canyon, mountain gorge, canoeing and rapids…this girl, long hair, it's all tangled and it's full of like acorns, bits of wood, husks, like beads threaded. Living in the gorges like a nature spirit, I see through the centuries, popping up, always this earth presence, a good way to live, camouflaged, in touch with the flora of the forest, wolf skin, Blue Cloud wearing wolf skin, says it's good to wear wolf's skin. To hunt like a wolf… to be invisibly, it's the invisible worlds…'

' Autumn leaves in the woods, forest. She is running through, the nature child, hair is all tangled'

'It's the healing feminine presence as Lone Wolf goes rushing down through the gorges in the canoe… Blue Cloud is wrapped in wolf skin, with knots in her hair, making potions, making medicine, medicine woman… Then the canoe is smashed on the rocks and Lone Wolf needs mending. It's Blue Cloud… medicine… But Blue Cloud is in hiding, hiding in the woods because she's been spurned, she's been rendered mad, it's the warriors, cast her aside… This is the great sadness and the poison… This hidden earth spirit needs reinstating… … Restore the wolf skin… She's had to cloak herself in wolf skin, unloved by all accounts, but it's the protection and her tenderness wasn't valued… A long history of female oppression, it's a journalist that can write about it but it doesn't end, it's a struggle for reinstating the feminine, locus, the healing will come from there, Frances just wants to say the wolf skin is just a protective cover…

the forces of devastation and destruction and desecration… Like Joan of Arc had to put on protective armour, the small voices which she was honouring … There are a lot of ladies with unfinished business… In reality the divine feminine has had to be hidden, it's been desecrated, despised, fraughted… Blue Cloud is a medicine woman and she is shouting… the blue cloud with the silver lining… free the woman, that's the message, free… Not only the healing the man but healing of the warrior, all women must be free and then we can paddle the canoe safely, safely through the torrents, down the gorges, over the rocks, into the caverns with the green trailing ivy vines. This is the story of Adam and Eve, this being told by Blue Cloud…

Blue Cloud's very sad in the countries where the boys are valued more than the girls all over the world… In so far as you close your hearts to the cries of the wolf skin, you deny the mother, mother Eve, you deny the earth, you deny your birth right, you deny God, you deny Jesus, you deny Buddha, you deny the Great Spirit and the wolf skin woman is the injured woman, the injured healer, the medicine woman who is cast aside… reinstate her; you can't go to the stars without her… Seven bridges, seven bridges we shall cross, and at the seventh there will be blue clouds, silver lined and the sun will shine through…

24/02/15

The Terrence Higgins Trust; a big flowering tree; keep it flowering keep it alive, keep it blossoming… sunshine, sunny days, keep it alive and blossoming, enjoy… When you light a flame you have to keep it alight, it can be easily snuffed out, we have to monitor it, tend it, protect it, like an Olympic flame we see how that travels all over the world, carefully tendered, passed lovingly from hand to hand…

It's a big symbol that… So you can light a flame and kindle an awareness but you have to feed it and keep it alive and growing so it will eventually be apparent, be a great blaze, will never die, the light will continue, gets to a threshold of brightness and then it can never be extinguished but until that point it's vulnerable. So for those that hear it's important to fan it, to blow…'

'Woshika, Woshika a little dancing boy, Woshika… this Woshika is looking at me with large eyes and is full of gratitude, he says even a short life can be blessed, is a source of joy and wonder. Everything that lives is holy.'

24/03/2015

'There's this group of people looking down at us, like bonneted ladies, Salvation Army. It's the whole world in their hands, to save or to be midwives to the birth of bringing Jonah forth out of the whale. Giving birth to the world, they're midwives, midwives of the future, Mary, Miriam, Martha, the bonneted ladies…'

'There's this nursery, we're being schooled, infants… most of us haven't yet been born'

'Tellurian, an epoch Tellurian… distance, this epoch… if that's where the switch was made, change, change of clothes, Tellurian… slate grey shiny like graphite, like metal, silvery grey dark, something to do with communication… concerned… concertinaed… like an accordion, layers finely folded… an image of a seal, sea lion, sea creature, very sleek, completely at home, completely adapted, happy… this strange hybrid creature like a mixture of all creatures, parrot head, claws, a bizarre concoction, try to do everything, this is a travesty, a lot of miss-fits. wipe the slate clean, back to the drawing board, this thread of steel, the thread running through it, it's pulling us forward…'

' An embryonic form, like a chrysalis in a cocoon, all these permutations going on like a great alchemic melting pot for centuries, aeons, the transformation, this is where the ignorance, it doesn't know what it's going to be, it can't… it's multi-potential, there are many interested parties, parents you might call them, which way is it going to go, from within there are brief flashes of inspiration, there's knowing, there's consciousness there, illumination. There is a self, initial intention, there is a beginning of a self-creating entity, cells, units, and they're focusing. That energy is forming a nucleus of knowledge and it's determining a form, a shape of things to come… and the parents are watching, waiting, how will it evolve? How will it emerge? They can wish, they can encourage with their thoughts and the illuminated cells are receptive, they intuit, they feel the urge, the pull to draw them to a particular form, a particular way of being. There are many embryonic forces…'

'Think of the story of Sleeping Beauty and the fairies that were called at her birth and the fairy that was not noted and his intention was slighted so there was some disharmony but the ill effects were mitigated, the result was a delay, was a stasis, time asleep, delay in the awakening, it's the prince of peace who gave the kiss, this is the Christos. The prince- he woke the sleeping beauty and it was the marriage of heaven and earth… Time, time is now… he is there… daughters of earth and the sons… the sons of space…'

'This chrysalis spinning on its stalk, spinning faster and faster, its vibrational rate increasing as the metamorphoses are completing, spinning increases and the creature is wriggling, restless, perturbed, writhing. A lot of disturbance as it breaks open, there's a break through, splits asunder, this new form emerges'

' the head of a lion, the talons of an eagle, the wings of a dove and the heart of a saviour… a new man… sweep the yard clean to prepare a place, to prepare for the birth, the emergence of the new man depends on the preparation, the clearing of the ground, of the old ways, the purging, take a new broom and sweep clean… prepare the way'

21/04/2015

' a sensation of a baby being born, the conduit of the parent, the mother and the child and something beyond compelling that child, through the mother, a clear lineage or link… Springtime, the coming into bud, the bringing forth of the dormant buds after wintering when they'd gone back to refresh, to sleep, to consolidate their energies. The spring is bringing forth new life, it's a continuity from source, but there's a possibility of new form, new shape and colour, new invigoration and the whole tree, the whole plant can change its shape. The nurturing of the new buds with the new blooms. Every new child is an opportunity and the wise parent observes and nurtures but allows for change and origination for moving away from the parent stock, change of form, change of shape, of direction, which is good…'

the image of an omelette, all the eggs have gone into it, a homogeneous mix, skilful cook, separate from the eggs, we've raised the chickens, all the lineages, there's all varieties gone into this omelette'

'kites, the kites harnessing the winds, energy to fly but the string is still attached. The kite maker is letting out the string, shortening the line, pulling it back, letting it go, helping to harness the wind'

'I have the diamond; it's like a great multifaceted… each turning of the lathe. Diana and a flower seller holding all these strands'

' the curator of the museum; he knows every artefact and its origins and its connection to the whole. He knows where it sits, he has a large building, a large enterprise to maintain more objects, artefacts are being brought in, others are being laid aside and rested and the great public comes and views, interest in a particular period, particular epoch. The curator holds it all in his mind and the information has been recorded into a data base, all can access it'

' images of carpets and tapestry, it's the weaving and construction, the cross threads, spinning wheels'

' It's to do with television, Baird, the long road, winding road. It's coloured, I see it in the science museum, the origin of television, all the history of the development, the chrome colour… Now there's not a home without a television almost. The development is the work of many, many minds. One maybe brought forward the concept into fruition and then it became a reality… But the concept, where was it? Where is it? Spinning out in space here there everywhere was always there. It's like number paintings, it's the matrix that the artist is brushing one pixel at a time, brings it to life then turns the page and there's a new painting to bring forth, to give birth again and again'

28/07/2015

it's as if the Ganges is being fed off into large lakes and dry areas, catchment, large areas of bare earth becoming pools'

'Abraham Lincoln like a great bird, a great vulture flying over India, over the Ganges with sky burials in the sky. Then the vultures clean the bones of the dead, clearing away all the decay, all the corruption of the flesh, leaving the place pristine, only the white bones… Abraham Lincoln equality, all men are created equal and in death whatever cast, whatever the status has been in life, all that remains is identical bones… All men are born equal; no one has right to any more than any other' *'there's a great shake-up coming to India and it has a connection to these pools being taken off the Ganges... seismic activity'*

'enormous wealth in the hands of a few in India, power, pictures of the army taking over and the suffering, the flushing out of all the old structures... this strong sense of the shaking up of the old structures which is very resistant to change... like a great avalanche'

'in a large airport, waiting, it's a control tower'

'... There's something blue, like the star of David, a prayer shawl, a flag... Nazarene... None of this is sustainable... I've got a fence around a lawn, fences can be taken down, fences are not permanent structures, they can be taken down'

'the words... "There is a green hill far away without a city wall" That should be Jerusalem... no walls, no fences...'

'This image of lots of airmail letters, writing, Pan Am, the whole world encompassed with wings and airmail, the carrying of messages, the crossing of boundaries, the traversing of time lines, the whole Earth circumscribed by flight. Then shall the Earth be full of the knowledge of God as the waters cover the sea, all lands are one land, all times are one time, all is now'

MERCURY EXPERIMENT

21/11/2013

'We're not hiding from you, you can sense us everywhere. We are the wind, the rustle of the leaves in the trees; the rain on your face is us touching you… We are in the music you listen to and the art you look at… Don't think of us as just people or entities…'

28/11/2013

wonderful to spend an evening like this with you'

'The seeds of time, don't waste them, plant them wisely'

05/12/2013

'There's a lot of preparation to do and we must have patience before we take the fruits. Our intention to bring forward evidence and the wonderful opportunity that presents is important work. We need to hold that focus as it gives a connection and they can get through'

'Seven walls to cross'

'Have to travel down many corridors of perception before you can perceive us as we truly are'

08/05/2014

'- A question Liz that you have, not about this group or this room but perhaps a deeper question… is there something you always wish to know?'

Liz… 'Well the truth!!!!…'

'There are many truths'

Liz… 'What it really is, what it's all really about'

'It is all about love… that is all that matters'

Liz… 'What has gone wrong with the development of mankind, that they've misconstrued love in such a way?'

'Nothing has gone wrong. It is sometimes hard for you on this plane to see the bigger picture. Everything is as it should be, it is part of the development of the human soul and all is not straight but sometimes twists and turns but there is nothing to fear, all is good'

Liz… 'What about the appearance of cruelty and war and aggression, how does that…'

'This is not an issue of the soul but of the body. It is the nature of things. When you realise that your soul and your body are not the same it will allow you to understand that the body, the stuff of matter, is denser and has a part of this heaviness sometimes what you would call negativity can manifest as cruelty and as war, but always God, there is no separation. You are not your body, you are just light, we are all just light. There have always been wars and there will always be conflict but this is a part of the learning. There are many higher realms than this where these things no longer happen but this is your school and sometimes even though you do not wish to go to school it is in your best interest…

29/05/2014

'Hark… the great shinning… blades of grass blazing with gold… he's trying to convey… the lambs again; feed my lambs… woven basket, a basket of grasses and rushes… Moses and ….the word of the prophets… I ask who's there and I get Leslie… I ask for a message and just get plain brown wrapping paper, keeping it simple…'

10/07/2014

'An assembly of friends… It doesn't matter you don't have to individualise them'

'All these people, why they don't need to individualise? That the uniform thing and the response to all of them underneath the thing that links them all is love, it's like a flower, and that's the thing, it's the experience, that's the only thing that's important, the experience, that unifying joining thread on which they're spun, on which they cleave and how they can come back as a unified thread. That's the only message, that's the only response, beyond that the rest is trivia, it's illusion, gossamer, the true essence, the nectar is the love'

23/07/2014

Pearly gates… This is heaven on earth… Contrast with pearly gates and the Pearl Harbour attacks… It's the same energy… Like the energy that gets you to the pearly gates can also create something like Pearl Harbour… It's a choice… A balance between right and left'

31/07/2014

It's Silver, talking about clouds and silver linings… Kites, strings…'

This is Silver, this is where it comes from, and where the kites are flying, it's drawn down the string, hold onto the string, watch the kite bobbing about in the clouds, like the lightening conductor drawing down this brilliance of light, inspiration, it comes from the shining one… All sons of the universe, they're all the shining ones, beings of light. We act like the lightening conductors, draw down their light; penetrate the earth, that's our purpose, so the earth is impregnated with light… This great colony of bees, this community of bees, making the nectar, taking the nectar, feeding it to the next generation'

'It's a bit like the snake shedding his skin, so many times, each of these is like the generations that fall away, new generation, new energies, then again the skin sheds off for a new generation. The new one continues but it's all one being, the skin disintegrates and is absorbed into the earth, the snake keeps going, following the passage of time'

'If I take the scales off your eyes, you will be blind if it's done too soon, but in the fullness of time the scales will fall away and then you will see and you will be seen… There are so many that have fallen by the wayside because the time wasn't right, it was too soon, timing is crucial'

'And when you wake up you won't want to sleep again, but it's a blinding day and you have to be ready, it's the light within us all… But my light is gentle and not to be feared, it's the safe way, like the slow way through the generations… Peter, it's Peter… That's all'

<u>14/08/2014</u>

Jigsaw… feels like a three dimensional jigsaw… citadel, rooftops, spires, castles, places of worship, places that control'

'It's the thread again, the total thread, drama of dreams, weaving together, binding all these pieces. Then the picture is the city of light, the citadel is the central, the nerve centre, the centre of consciousness, the throne. ... This is the picture that they are building, this is the heaven on earth, it's what we should be looking at'

21/08/2014

Seamless... Without a seam, the two realities... Crows, flocks of ravens and crows... Just glad to be here, over the land the birds, flocks of birds and then the sea lions under the ice, streaming along... The various habitats, the elements, each at home, in its element and seamless, the realities, one. They blend under a sheet, a seamless sheet of reality... Streamlined...'

28/08/2014

'The incredible witness'

'The sun dance, the Indian dance for dreams... long leather straps, dried skin, threads made of skin, the umbilicus, the navel'

'It's the master architect... bricks... building blocks, like in a cave, the stone marble, materials of the earth build up a picture, the builders, they work with bricks, units of earth, rock, mortar and brick... the same designs, patterns... change is subtle over civilizations, becomes the common thread, the common thread is the architect'

'Vibration is a sound... a house that is fit for a king is singing the right tune'

18/09/2014

skirts of the earth they're so beautiful… the great distance, the blue, the green and the white… it's the one earth… we're holding onto the unity… the name Gordon………. from our perspective it's all a playground…'

'A highland kilt, beret, bag pipes… a lot of concern, the clans… they're saying one island, no change… something about Culloden, these are the old battles… it's a universal perspective, looking through a telescope puts things into perspective, gives you a bigger picture… dancing on the graves, the old battles…'

'Looking at this wall, it's Hadrian's wall… I'm just seeing the mountain, Caledonian mountain rising up out of the sea, this great… all joined up, once it was all joined, the whole continent, there was… like a great buffalo, like a great animal coming out of the sea, this great body of land open for all, shining, gleaming, great mountain ranges, volcanic, granite… who does it belong to? The whales and the dolphins… they have more sense… monkeys squabble… great dragon rising up out of the sea, sleeping, gleaming, should all be cherished as one earth, one great ball, hold in the hands… not to be carved up, not to be divided, to be shared… it's like a string of pearls, all the islands of the earth, all the tracts of land held by a thread, all joined… all one earth… this playground was given to all, this theatre and the diamond sky, it's safe, run a fence around it, a net, Indra's net…'

'It's the theatricals of this species in our theatre… it's not to be taken too seriously… shadow plays… this is like a black diamond, multi-faceted stone… penetrating reality, behind them the vast skirts of the earth they're so beautiful… the great distance, the blue, the green and the white… it's the one earth… we're holding onto the unity…

'If you look at them under a microscope they seem very fixed, that resolution, but without the microscope all things are visible... for those under the lens, to them it's every day, it's real, it's well defined...'

shining lights, this is the surface play, the shadow theatres... it might not seem it for the mortals caught up in it...'

16/10/2014

'The grey doves that nestle in my breast... want to hold them... warm in my heart... I've tied knots in my belt, a cord belt, to remind me, a kindness...'

'Something to do with penitence and remembering... remembering the faults and correcting them, to perfect, bringing them to mind in order to transmute them to do better next time... to bring to mind all the impediments... nurse things that stand in the way with kindness and simplicity... and to sincerely wish to change... and the harshness, the cold helps to bring it to mind, knots to sharpen, to resolve... When things are easy and comfortable the incentive to change isn't sharp... When things are difficult and uncomfortable the resolve sharpens...'

30/10/2014

'Christos... Jesus's miracles all being much simpler... which world you pitch your activity in, you relate to the Christos,
the Christ level, it's just very simple, it's where you have your... where you pitch your activity in... Your desire in the make believe, dream world, mundane... of the greater reality... just a shift of focus... It's the teaching... because children, they've not fixed their mind yet, their focus can be guided to be able to perceive and draw on the sun and the Christos'

'I have an image of a building seven stories high… It's like looking at a belisha beacon, different colours; I think this is like going up, pitching your level… I'm looking out of the top of the building trying to home in on a cave… the cave seems to be made of mud, a brown cave, sort of earth… Dark brown people, sun baked… Seems to be a civilization like Aztec, Indians, Amazonian… They have nothing, no cloths; they have this amazing communication like telepathy. They all seem to be doing different things but it is all connected, earth caves, dugouts… The Earth is important to them. I've got trees, not a lemon but similar… I like these people, it's like their life is a smile… Now I seem to have gone into a land of… it's very beautiful but slightly different, Eskimos… That way of living, as one with the Earth… I need to come back to it; you see they had their computers in their heads… We've weakened the connection; we've put it outside ourselves… We need to get it back on the inside… I got the image, all those bubbles, they got too many and fragmented, then the ability to coalesce into one larger bubble is much weaker, it's weakened. If they remained fewer, more robust,

not fragmented so much, stronger inside, then the coalescing into one big one is much stronger, more enduring… Fragmentation weakens ability…'

25/11/2014

'Distant bridges… there is no distance… filled with the void. The image of an ostrich egg and this great marble, and the black diamond, but this is the infinity, the cosmic cake. Each of us is seeded in it and we seed it. It's an infinite regression…. holographic image of an infinite series of Russian dolls, every little speck, every little particle is the whole of the void and the whole is filled and the significance of the black diamond is a diamond is prismatic, reflects all light, all the colours, the black absorbs all and you have this infinite movement out and radiant and inwards and back through it.

It's the breath in and the breath out, total cosmic breath, movement involution and evolution, what evolves, devolves, again and again and again…'

Behind all phenomena, which is the painting is this incredible light, which is the blank canvas, out of which all comes and that light is still shining through every single moment. Every moment of your life is valuable, is essential and that essential life is in every single phenomena and every moment. It's like we are getting back to the blank canvas but through all phenomena the incredible whiteness and blackness of this original blank canvas, the origin is shining through and that is the power. All phenomena is diluted in it, it's weaker and it's hard for us to take the full strength but just to be aware that locked into every moment and every phenomena, every little blade of grass we meet is the brilliance of this light shining from the blank canvas, the origin before it was painted…

02/12/2014

'A peacock's feather, wisdom, those colours of wisdom and a flash of emerald… I think it's locked into matter again, this incredible wisdom, it's there in the dense darkness of the material man. Even in the dugouts of war there's the reflection in the puddle, passing glory, bat's wing, bird's wing, butterfly wing, dragonfly wing, this gleam. It's the colours of the Green Tara, the blue and green, this earth wisdom, this reflection, it's the reminder… The passing beauty glints and gleams, it's to remind, to remember that these are the links, they're like keys, you turn it and it opens, it's Pandora's box, the jewels, the seven jewels, it's a trigger these little gems that in the everyday appear but they are triggers to deeper truths and everyone will open to link to the original blank canvas..'

'Hawk… Hawkeye, he's just observing, there to have an overview, scan from a perspective, a higher perspective but the civilizations come and go, it's the blink of an eye. From the ground it seems slow, get caught up in the present and temporal, it's not important, a lot of *what happens is gone in a blink… It's food for the gods, the taste, send it up, what we've managed to distil from this murky perspective, the denseness of matter, the locked in state, to unlock the jewel so it has a special flavour, the iridescence when it is released that's what you take back, that's what is important. It's very small, most of it is trash, it's like the nugget, the goodness from the food we eat, small compared to the dross waste that goes out but it's that that's transmuted, that's distilled through the human consciousness, that's returned. It has this flash, this iridescence that becomes part of the painting, that's recorded…'*

'That's what is the important work of a lifetime, to distil the quintessential, the essence what is the root of every experience and to stir it into the stew. Proof of God, so each individual acts like a diamond, a prism focusing and then distilling and dispersing clear radiant colours, the finer detail, the essential nature is reflected back… it takes a new gleam, the whole desire, reflections of reflections of reflections… It's another way of putting it, it's the fine tuning, as the energy gets dispersed into denser and denser pools at each level, the clear note, the original note must be found. That's the link, that's the thread; draw the whole web back inwards into itself, Indra's Net… When you're lost in the dark it's an agony to get back to the origin, to the light, it means finding that thread, that nerve, that connection which is the portal, then the darkness becomes light…'

'He's from a higher perspective; it's just a gigantic and wonderful experiment… I just get a sense now of seeing through a myriad of forms, through snakes, swaying head, giraffe, the fruits on the bush, through perception, through all those myriad eruptions, different ways of being, seeing, the experience is mind boggling, a higher level…'

'As a created being it's almost impossible to perceive the levels of the creator beyond the whole because of our confines. To break through

into the vision, into the mind, the being of the whole, just a glimpse, it is so enormous that as a created being we can only be in awe of the magnificence...'

09/12/2014

'The grey wolf again, the skein and the Golden Fleece, the thread chasing after it... it's joyous... This is Mother Earth and the golden skein from the Golden Fleece, the wool is the thread, the consciousness that's holding all the interludes, all phenomena together, these great spaces, the seven hills... Over the hills is the golden city of Jerusalem... The grey wolf seems to have become a grey clothed monk, a monk with a grey cloak'

'The seven hills are not just temporal epochs but they're also stations within the body, within the physical being... And Jerusalem has something to do with where we are now and that's the Christos, that's the epoch'

'sheep with wagging tails...'

'an amazing honeycomb, it's like a bee hive with all the cells interconnected, it's golden again, golden honeycomb. All the cells interconnecting a community, an incredible hive of activity

that community interconnectedness, again that's related to the skein, golden thread which is the complexity of the weaving, that is your basket'

'This honeycomb, each cell contains a little unit of consciousness, a little unit of life but they're all interconnected and the whole functions as one great universal consciousness and when the walls are broken down there is just the honey, the golden honey and that's the ambrosia, that's the nectar for the gods... that's the clear golden liquid, that's our food, it's the pure golden essence of consciousness reflecting the sunlight, the Christos, that's our rightful food, that's our rightful sustenance'

'That's the significance of feed my sheep, is the food, is this essential, the gold of consciousness, the Christ consciousness, is that essence and that source to be fed to each unit, each unit of consciousness, individual consciousness and that will help each to grow to its rightful place in the kingdom, the kingdom of heaven and the kingdom of heaven is the kingdom of heaven on Earth'

'Now I come back to the roses that are growing in the garden in abundance even though it's winter, these are the heart roses'

'I have this image of the golden crown... I've been given a cloak, purple and it's being placed around my shoulders, it's a taste...'

'I feel that what has been said is that we are all the rightful heirs to the kingdom but to claim that throne there is a lonely journey in the mist where all signposts are lost in the sign-less land, great vast steps and the seven hills and to lead into the unknown, to be prepared, to perceiver in the face of not knowing, in the blizzard, you're coming through, this journey into light but to retain the kingdom requires breaking down the walls of the familiar, letting go, stepping into the unknown. It's an act of courage but the golden skein, the golden thread, that thread of consciousness carries you

through and leads you to the light, to Jerusalem, to the kingdom, to your throne and the crown... I have this final image of the rose with thorns, that the journey is not without thorns...'

06/12/2014

to survive in this world you need the strength and severity of the tiger, this eye close to the track and trail, the soft belly, the softness to procreate, to bond, to befriend, to love... Tracks in the snow almost obliterated, tread lightly...'

20/01/2015

round gold plates, like the sun, a ritual, lighting a candle for the birthday boy, one candle. These gold plates are for the offering,

Footsteps... behind the footsteps there's a circuitous route. They're going back on themselves leading through this terrain. this is the shaman path.

'like the Hansel and Gretel story, that sweet house, the distraction takes you off the path, sets up a trap, the honey trap. It's a caution not to be seduced by being very hungry. A safe familiar gingerbread house, it's a honey trap'

'amulets, beads, all the paraphernalia of the shamanistic path but looking beyond there's a deep pool just going towards the mountains, that's where you should be setting your sights, this deep crystal pool, the clarity, just don't get caught up with all that ritual and paraphernalia. It's the pure clear water that's to drink. I'm just holding onto that image of the crystal clarity, that great pool of water'

'see the light in the candle stick again. you can use the light of the candle flame in the same way'

servants, ready to serve. It's the plates, the service, it's the gold plates of the service and it's the feeding of the lambs. That's what's the significance of the gold plates, gold plates is the golden service, the service of the heart of gold to purify that heart, to get to the crystal waters, the cleansing, the purification'

'It's only a reflection of the master, the master mind behind the gold plates, an image, the signs are everywhere, there are the hints, the *tender reminders that a force and power behind the paraphernalia, behind all images, all the imaginings, all the phenomena, all the magic and mystery. The gold plates of service are a simple reminder of the great pure love, the joy, the abundance, the creative spirit'*

'It's the yearly reminders, the birthdays, that what is born will die, that behind that is the unborn and in that which is born, which dies is also the unborn. The birthday, it's to remind that behind all phenomena, changing phenomena, is the reality of the unborn, uncreated, that which is the truth and to have a glimpse of it you have to find your way to the crystal water in the high hills and these are the words… Who shall ascend the hill of the Lord and who should stand in his holy place, he who has clean hands and a pure heart who does not lift up his soul to what is false…'

(Liz was quoting from psalm 24)

'The years are flying past all at different speeds but they are an illusion, there is no time, all time is one time, all is one. Hannah just wants to remind that the candles of the birthday boy are just to remind of the truth that that which is born dies and that beyond all birth and death is the one, the ineffable, the true light, without name, without form, that which is'

' it's taste and see and the taste is the drinking of this deep, deep water of life, that crystal water is the water and if you drink this water you drink deeply and never go thirsty again. You have to follow that path into the wilderness through the wild places, the pure places avoiding the honey trap. The austere hills, the mountains where the origin is the waters, untainted, the source, go there and drink'

'there's a quality to this water, this pathway in this physical reality that registers the essence, this essential truth that allows it to be recorded in the heart, that allows it to be seen more directly, more deeply, to penetrate. It's an equity of focus that if you get it while

you are here it's lasting, can never be taken away. It's the opening of the doorway to the never ending stairs…'

03/02/2015

'Silver sent Sheila. She's crossing the bridges, sending her love, safe, safe now. It is like….a birthday, joyful. Say goodbye - it's not forever…. terrified at first……there's a sound, she was terrified; it's all right now……it's like a great assembly of people.

'It's the joy of the gathering, the confluence of many rivers coming together that's the joy of the gathering. It's like the many rivers coming together, all the strands, so many people in life we meet sometimes just momentarily, passing by contact and that contact is established. It's a network and the presence remains and that connected network is established and at some point all those trickles, strands come together and shine, form a great confluence, they come together in awareness, it's like the many arteries and blood vessels and fibres that make up the eye all coming together to create vision, a

great mess but the end result is seeing. We see through the eyes of many, through the eyes of others, all eyes become the one great seeing, individual eyes become the sight, the seeing of the see. A

great consciousness of being shared, shared feeling, the one, made of many and the many are one, always the one, the eye and the I, the I am'

'Terrified dreams, terrified projections and they turn and they all come home to me, I am the source, I am the whole, I am the son'

17/02/2015

Verdant, it's the green again, verdant pastures… this sense of resurrection, new life, new vitality of the Earth, the green shoots, the importance, the cherishing of maintaining, of nourishing, regenerating new green growth and they want to protect the health, that's good. It's the rebirthing; it's also called the emerald isle…'

'You have to hold on to the hope, hope is the rope, it will pull us into the future, nearer to the green future'

To hold on to the hope and the mindless ones will fall behind, the predominant urge is towards growth and the greening and those that fall short of that to mindless savagery just decay, fall away because the thrust is towards the new growth and the greening and the hope that's pulling us along and upwards and into the new age… so join the growth and leave the prison behind'

'fight the good fight, the sense of there being an army of helpers poised and ready there to bring the dream into being, to guide, to inspire, to fire the arrow into the future, the great greening of the Earth reality. A body, an army of helpers, diamond… We are all here just waiting, poised… I get a sense of some impending action… The reservoir of energy raining down on the Earth, over the houses, green, flowers… awakening'

03/03/2015

' a gown, a ceremony or coronation, crown… these linked hearts… an eternity ring… this picture of railings and things being fenced in, all very official and proper. The feeling is the love is outside all, much greater, expansive… Love is greater than all this, transcends it, the pomp and the glory…'

'a sort of love story, someone who had a very ordered and grand life but the most important thing was very simple and that was this love… just wanted to show that this love, that out of everything that was the best, the thing that shone… the garden, the rest is grey paving stones… pretentions…'

Daphne, pointing to the night stars, dazzling, the great universe, the great mystery… seek and ye shall find… it's an endless adventure, outward and inward at the same time, what you see outwards in the stars and the universe is just a mirror of what is your side. It's all there, dimensionless, diamond'

31/03/2015

'…a sculpture, Cleopatra's Needle… the contrast of the sculptures of Moreau with Wordsworth's poem upon Westminster Bridge… this contrast of the sublime and the ugly, ridiculous war, the gas, the struggling bodies and then the uplifted poem on the bridge… two sides of the coin'

'this enormous chess board and the sense that living life is like playing a game, taking on the different parts or moves but ultimately is to maintain the king, majesty. To hold onto the majestic, that feeling of majesty, of sovereignty in whatever you do. Any game, any part of a game, it's all a game but the important thing is to hold onto the king, your majesty, a supreme player, that's what I am, that's who you are, that's the I, all the others are fragments of it and they're moving only to defend, to bring its final position, the sole survivor, the majesty. All the other players are moving, the king is still, the king is the witness to all those players, acting out their parts'

'I have this great wave of pity, this unendurable suffering, I just say take her to the light, offer it as a gift, no rhyme or reason, it's the dark side of experience'

'Sheila's sowing silk parachutes to lift people up into the light when they are stuck, they begin to see the light, they have a parachute of gossamer like silk, very light, fills with the buoyancy of air, can take them to the islands for healing'

'flying like a great goose, I get the feeling of this circadian clock going round and round… these rotations are important… tick tock'

'gravity, it's spiralling down… a vortex… image of a great tree blossoming, tree full of birds and creatures…

' great nets made of knotted rope used to be full of shiny silver fish… trawling…'

'There are so many connections but there's only one sea… so many connections but one fisherman…'

07/04/2015

'It's a Van de Graaff generator, it's got this great crystal, spark igniting… Not here to entertain, we have the truth, raven, raven glass… This is the whole universe, stargate, this great crystal, crystallised structure held, gliding through space, all happening simultaneously… Slipping through the space… The nodes connection point… Galileo, swinging through the spaces, contact all times… Can take a fraction, it's not of time… Time's an illusion, if you were talking Swiss cheese… Crystallisation is time and space, fractals growing, continue, it's dimensionless, throw away the rulers and compasses… Slip through the nodes and glide like a fish, swim in the sea… Crack, it's a spark in this crack of ice, ice crack… It's as if we strike a match in the night, it's ghostly illumination, looks fixed, only a chunk, just endless reflections… You try and hold the wind in the palm of your hand… The idea of a snake, it's swallowing its own tail…'

stop asking questions, jump right in the sea, you have to be there to know it… Contemplate, … Easy… Swiss cheese, just look through the hole… dive into the sky'

'Crossword puzzle and the answers are upside down… clues… anagrams… these are just temporary devices for holding the mind, for fascinating the mind… The real work, the true seeing is underneath this going on in the spaces, behind, the back of the page… Real seeing is behind so don't get too caught up in the crossword puzzle, everything's known…'

'Stellar information… hands washing over… over and out'

14/04/2015

''Stepping stones……there's countless points of reference, countless beings, all pointing, all the footsteps on the path, all the cues, the signs. So where do we look? Well, in ourselves, it's our pointing, our speaking, our interpretation…

"so many minds, a crowd; it's like a gardener's sweet peas… the picture of Mendel… the mutation…. to get the clear message is not too easy, the light trying to form a strong stalk, a strong conductor, a conduit, it'll come , this subject has so many

influences, so many conditions, but there's some mind optimum, some confluences and then the conduit will flow very clear and true, channelling… yes, just lay back and let it happen, to be ready at the right time. Rubicon, again the rightness evolves the threshold… Once you've got over the hump it's clear sailing and there's a big effort to help. I sense they are all smiling and waving, very pleased.

'Back in the garden of Earthly delights…'

12/05/2015

'image of a green close knit jumper unravelling'

'this cantilever… it's to do with the bridge, this incredible cantilever structure, cross pieces, someone to do with engineering. Pylons… very ornate structures and I get the feeling all this work is wasted… structures collapsing… it's his own invention. He's devastated when his structures are destroyed… You think that these structures are very permanent, so carefully constructed, intricate… but everything that's been destroyed can be built again, the pattern is there. Once you have a pattern it's imprinted and the physical structure doesn't… it's neither here nor there, the pattern can be created again and again… It's the same with the knitting, there's the jumper that's unravelled but if you know how to knit you can knit it again, the pattern… that's the value of patenting, you patent the pattern so even though the physical body breaks down and deteriorates the pattern patent is still there, you can come back to it any time… Same with the pastoral idyll that was a good life style, a patent pattern, it's there, leave it behind, it can be recreated any time'

19/05/2015

'a strong sense of the forest, woodlice and creatures… It's a good place to be… There's your mouse, long tail…'

' this pattern like shingles or like the way feathers are layered on each other, a shelter, it's a pattern in nature like pine cones, it's the overlapping layers, a way of keeping out the rain, a protection, shells, scales, husks… I now have a sense of pushing up through the soil like a mushroom and there you have on the cap of the mushroom the scales… A sense of upheavals and the sense of the importance of shelter, to trust the Earth and the safe places and follow the patterns of nature, sustainability, close to the soil, close to the earth, the way of the forest…'

'a face like a great Aztec or Mien leader. there was an emphasis that in building up the big structures they'd lost the sense of the Earth… emphasising the importance of going back to fundamentals… great cities, great edifices are crumbling, covered in flies, nature is taking over…'

'We've got so much technology, so much edifice… as all edifices it's vulnerable, Earth changes, we need to learn to survive, go back to basics…'

'Christabel is showing me the rainbow colours in her weaving because the rainbow wishes a promise, hope, salvation…'

'a strange sense of tunnelling in the Moon… Cordalite… It's a beautiful shell like a conch, perfect form…'

''I'm on a tobacco boat, lots of different people, looks like a connection with the slave trade, trading, it seems to be a connection with the West Indies, tobacco… A strong mixture of black and white people living simply… gold… I just left peace to all protagonists in this pageant, that's what it's like, a pageant… I'm looking up at the star now, I just end with peace that passes all understanding to all players, all images, all imaginings, all imagination, everything on both sides… peace..'

02/06/2015

'Equinox, a box, coffin… the coffin is like a doorway, the shape of the coffin is like the hull of a boat. That wooden shape that you think is a box, the end, the final container, is actually like a doorway. It is like the hull of a boat taking us into a sea, into new lands, a voyage, a journey, into exploration and then we have these marvellous discoveries, to learn new ways of being… I've been given the key to unlock the coffin. What we see as finality is infinite; it's only opening doors, going from room to room'

'image of a great tree and the branches are spreading out and the twigs on the end are growing, keeps growing, spreading out and out and out, tendrils going out and out and out, it's endless growth. It's an image of fractals, dimensions, infinite dimensions…'

'The image of the seed planted in the fertile soil of this Earth, this planet, this tree grows and emerges this growth. It starts here, this is the fertile Earth and this seed, we are emerging from this seed, a green shoot at first, it's hard to see what it's like. This sense of it spreading, almost like looking at a crack that's spreading through a sheet of ice… That's an interesting image in the finality of it, the crack expands and expands and expands across the ice sheet which breaks up and in the end is just the clear water until it freezes over again… these images are just ways of trying to understand the evolution of life, what life is'

'Garden child, Margarite… the child looks like Alice in Wonderland. this castle of cards, a pack of cards, big or small. She sees through the phenomenal nature of all creation, the dream, ultimately all aspects of her… Alice was very lonely in that realisation'

'It's like the Mad Hatter's tea party, a big table, they're reshaping reality, parallel shifting, keep at it… castles in the sky'

'Now see the relevance of it, it was the tune in, turn on, the psychedelic scene with the magic mushrooms, all of that, that was the beginning, it was to try and change the whole energy, paradigm shifting, that from that time it's evolved into the consciousness movement, the new age growth with techniques, a more slower development but it's this impulse to transform to get 10% of the world's population turned on, tuned in, shifted, evolved, a breakthrough. I want to ask the question… How do we do it? Can we help? Are we helping? There are people who have passed over who are more active now, in a better position, are working still, beaming down. This is like the satellite, you have a universal worldwide coverage, satellite transmission, that's the new age, you can get one message of inspiration through and it can get viral, beam down, tune in, broadcast worldwide, that's the way now… I think that's the new generation that are primed, ready to receive the transmission… I got this image of a ladder on the other side that those who passed over had to climb, it's ongoing… I get this image of a ship with the rigging, they're climbing up to the crow's nest, from there they can beam down and transmit. They have to get there first and they're getting there… This is important that we like many others on the ground are preparing ourselves, putting ourselves in the position to receive, reception needs earthing'

09/06/2015

We have a Garden of Eden here on Earth and it's underestimated. The power of recreation and how important these activities are, just having fun, enjoying'

'the importance of unstructured activity, the walks, outings… The word keeps coming back, kaleidoscope… I guess the kaleidoscope is just a restructuring all the time of the elements, the same elements, they're just being restructured, re-patterned'

'We bury the beautiful body, it's like the kaleidoscope, the elements have just all got shuffled around again, that beauty goes on, it's just reconfigured…'

'These collisions, things happen but life goes on in one way or another… The valuable recollections, times in the park, a peaceful time, autumn colours, cherish those moments, water under the bridge. By looking into the stream many reflections and the reflections aren't the real thing, the reflections are changing, the water is changing… everything is reconfigured… looking for what's constant. Pull all my pieces together to have some semblance of I, the I underneath it all'

'A difficult thing to maintain focus when you are so many… I can be the black bird, I can be the snow, all the reflections but in the physical world it's much easier to be one thing, to hold the focus, to sustain identity. Out here beyond I can be all the stars in the universe, all the stones in the sea... Where's my beginning, where's my end'

'Memorabilia is like ashes, most is like empty medals, bits of ribbon, they're not worth hanging onto, scraps, not important. The most important thing is the park... it's the quality of the enjoyment'

23/06/2015

Pied Piper of Hamlin, the story, of course the plague of rats, the town being plagued, becoming a pestilence and the Pied Piper appears and promises to rid the town of rats, ...ends ... the politicians and mayor won't pay him so he takes all the children off, he spirits them away... I guess there's a danger that we're losing the plot, we're not fulfilling our bargain, cleaning up. the Earth and there's a price to pay for that. The price is our future generations...'

14/07/2015

In the case of the caterpillar and the chrysalis... in the chrysalis it looks as though it's the dormant stage, nothing is happening, like it's inanimate, but things are happening inside and eventually, it may be a long time, the new spiritual being flies free. Like someone maybe who's been in a coma for a long time, it would seem as though that was a long dormant period but things are happening on the inner planes, finally there's a transformation and the spiritual being, that portion, is freed'

21/07/2015

'I don't think we can judge anyone, many we think are maverick, they're just shaking up the beliefs and establishment, playfully poking fun at beliefs and structures that are outmoded' 'from brother Michael to these old Zen monks of Japan in caves, they are quite crazy, their methods were, leading people to enlightenment, sometimes shock tactics, using paradoxes and imponderables turning the mind upside-down'

… yes the children, keep the lamps alight…'

'the association with old desks and school rooms, dusty old school rooms, teaching. I see these bright gardens and bright spaces with butterflies and underneath it is love, that's the barometer, the true teaching of richness of any experience if it puts you in touch with love, if it increases the love, if there is love there that's a good lesson. It can appear in the most unlikely places'

04/08/2015

'this web, it's like gossamer, like a net curtain, delicate, like a fisherman's net, fishers of men, between the two isles… deep sea

divers bringing up pearls… nuggets of wisdom… outward expression of the distillation of experience'

'Bright corn, ready to be harvested, bright grains… experience, harvest… we misrepresent experiences, this newspaper façade of images, of information, of pageant, stories, very superficial, sort of running on the surface noise, it's like mining for gold, panning for gold, big sieves, amongst the mud, the grains and the grains when sifted out of raw debris an ounce of gold… pounds of debris and an ounce of gold'

'silverman… a sense of silver coins… Sydney Silverman had a connection with abolition of hanging … the image of a hangman's rope in connection with justice, silver scales… the feeling of the struggle in this life to bring through these values, justice, all these things they seem to have to be fought for… again like gleaming droplets of gold amongst all the mire, pearl in the depths, to extract these, to bring out the essential in this mire of profanity which can be the mental noise of human existence is difficult to sustain, to sustain the effort, to clarify, to hold the vision, it needs to maintain the focus, that intention, once you've grasped the shining quality to hold on to the vision, to pursue it because it will lead to the truth'

'I'm wanting to ask what it's like to die, the next step. I have this feeling of this great sea of molten gold like stepping into the sea with the sunrise on it, the sun as it's rising it's spreading its gold over the whole sea, is like a molten furnace of gold and just the brightness and the wonderful goldenness is homing in and immersing me and you can surrender to it. It's the ultimate transition of Narcissus, from the I to the not I, yet still I, I am'

25/08/2015

'a slightly pungent smell like a grass, daisies, crushed daisies… It's like walking on eggshells… like the skin of the World, this shiny surface, feeling this

shining surface, this skin like a polished mirror and the inside is like the inside of the eyeball… When I ask them what does this image relate to? I was told the World… There's a sense of the syllables, the sounds… there's too much to tell… An instruction has been given but the words and meanings have been hidden but they are there for all to see, to hear… held within this daisy flower, very simple… I'm shown that having these places of power, hidden instruction is given, is revealed in the form of visions, in the form of seeing, hearing, and these teachings are for everyone to be shared. Don't dismiss them idly, understand that they are the whisperings of truth… sound being the vehicle for instruction and the dissemination of truth, sound in all its forms, vibration on the surface, the still surface reflects it, the eyeball of the World'

15/09/2015

'A worm… the worm that turned. The worm that can turn the tables, that can change the world. It turns the underground, it keeps the earth moving. The worm moves the Earth to all intents and purposes, the lowliest of creatures'

and grace having many meanings… by the grace of God and grace also being thankfulness, gratitude, gracias… grateful grace of the multitudes, the dust of the Earth, for the many that are also one…'

'I'm left with a chair and it's empty, I should sit on it'

29/09/2015

'David, it's the boy, David.'
'Nest of scorpions… I sense some bitterness'

'a green hill, a temple and the old man has picked up this bird, this heavy golden statue - he's set it free, it's a bird, it's flown away, that's how it should be… and his eyes have opened. It's as if he was tied to the treasure, this solid heavy… To him it represented a golden image, an object of worship, he converted it. Realisation is the key word. He'd imprisoned the real, stultified it, made a graven image of it and now he's set it free, he's realised its essential nature. That's the graven image of God, that's what we've done, the nest of scorpions. God is a living being, free, alive can't be pinned down, not to be worshiped, to be lived… The musical instrument has to be played, it's a fixed and solid object until a hand plucks the strings and the music dances forth, creation has wings… The music arises from the object according to the player' 'sheep grazing on the hillside. These sheep have golden fleeces, they're a commodity, no they're not for sale… Everything has its price but its true value is lost, its true value is not seen… Every living thing has become armoured with price tags and defences, the greed. Every living thing has become so fixed in its perceived commodity value, commodity price. Objects of trade, of admiration, constrained, captive. The true nature has been dimmed, over looked. It's not being seen for what it is only for what it's worth in terms of commodity value'

'Ashes… sack cloth and ashes, garments of repentance… I've seen what I've seen, I am what I am now as a great sea of gold and peace… in the end all is peace'

06/10/2015

'A skein of wool like a cat's cradle that seems to be going to the cave where the woman was, a princess… It's as if this woman is in charge of all wild things, it's like there are many faces, faces of many faces, she's sometimes known as a star… Also known as Diana the huntress… Astarte, a connection with Egypt and I have the moon goddess… The wool is the connective tissue, the link out of the tangled web. All things are held together and connected and the skein of wool acts as a pathway not to get lost, it winds and unwinds, it's used to trace the footsteps so the path isn't lost, to find a way back home… the home is not far way, it's where you are, there never was any distance, there's nowhere to go to get lost because you're always home, home is where you are and the skein of wool is just an illusory device to help you remember… She is the star to every wandering bark, she is the princess, she is the home, she is the heart, she is the queen of hearts and she's been with us all through history, Astarte... and she's also Tsultrim Allione, the girl's guide, Sudakini and Vajralila's guide... so I think it's women of the world unite your time has come, rebirth of the woman... I think I have Francis with me and she says... Well said... and that's the significance of the tigress, absolute mastery, noble bearing, supreme presence...'

20/10/2015

'you are indeed a twinkle in your father's eye but you need to feel the eye, to see through the eye in which you are a twinkle...'

'Ai Weh... Ai Weh a pathway of lapis lazuli, a turquoise leading to Ai Weh... Mounte, mounte of aman... There by the river and the tents are scattered, millions by the yellow river, washed down with a flood, I've noted, Ai Weh noted... Nothing is ever lost, it's like a mushroom, mycelium, the threads are all there and the fruit returns and returns every year... Why would you keep returning? It's the lapis lazuli, the treasure at the end of the rainbow, the promise of the treasure... So what is to be done with the treasure? Is it put away? Is it buried? Treasure is the food for gods... it's the treasure we take with us when we pass on, when we become gods. We are the gods; Ai Weh says we are the gods ... it's like a great egg that's cracked open, the egg is hatching, feathers coming out of it, peacocks, peahens, all the colours of the rainbow... there's no going back, only forward... He's shouting, he's come, he wants to get the message across, he's come with Ai Weh, ... the message is... he said it's love, there's no resistance now... It's like tsunami, a wave, a rush of energy spreads, it's almost like an aroma, spreading the message, it's seeping through the mycelium, the layers... that it comes in a rush and then percolates, it's a new wave... Ai Wey is a mountain of a man, he's been trying to say it with lapis lazuli, he will say it with lapis lazuli... That's all...'

03/11/2015

Of what shall we build the house?'

'this house, almost like a tent, made of silks that have rainbow patterns, colours painted on them in silk and this silk is spun from the humblest of creatures the worm, turquoise…'

'Image of these bubbles, bubbles have this filmy rainbow on the surface like in iridescent patterns on oily water, on an insect's wing, these delicate membranes… Of what shall we build our house?'

these silks again, embroidery silks, like walking down a path of sweet peas, very subtle pastel colours, scented, sheer artistry, the creation…'

'When you look at bubbles that are forming a bubble can engulf another bubble, they can coalesce and form a bigger bubble. These are just subtle manifestations of energy perceived by the eyes or it can be music for the ears, manifestations of energy, one soundwave being modulated by another, absorbing another waveform, another function of light, the sound of energy, energy forms absorbing, coalescing, mixing with others. We can interpret this in different ways according to our cultural beliefs, our conditioning, can see it as savagery, extinction, murder of one species by another one, erased by another, invasions, takeovers, assimilations. This is just the natural flow and transition and the creative patterning of energy in all its manifestations and it's all perfect, it's all how it is… Of what shall I build this house?'

'It's the mirage of phantasmagoria, moving, coalescing, shifting, shape changing, miracle. The patterns and the colours and the shapes and the sounds like clouds, changing, patterning and the bursting like bubbles…'

'lessons to be learnt from this falling snow, this great vast snowy dessert, wilderness, that in the middle there's absolute presence and fire lit in the middle of this snow and ice, and the wolf, the wind and the knife edge of survival sharpens the focus into the ice crystals, the meaning, the meaning of predation, of the predator and prey, it's attunement, that the one becomes exquisitely sensitive of the energy of the other'

'What we see as pain, suffering and cruelty in this world is just our interpretation of something we see as fixed which is in fact an energy construct, a waveform and if we saw it as music, patterns, iron filings in a field being moved, shifted in different ways forming different shapes, patterns, being absorbed, being individualised again, single note, single waveform and then bifurcating into a complex pattern and breaking up again, merging with a larger field pattern, all the time transforming. You see the objects as we see them of nature, in their true aspect of energy, the interactions, transitions and patternings can be understood, appreciated independent of our thinking, of our conditioned response, reaction'

'the lady in the silk kimono ... she's dancing. The kimono contains all the shapes and forms of all living things and around her are all created forms and the lion and the lamb are lying beside each other and are with her in friendship, there's no fear because all forms are understood for what they are and she's dancing the dance of creation and her name is Isis… That's all…'

10/11/2015

'attention to detail, every line, every expression, every stage of growth, every person, every transition is noted, is observed, is registered, is lovingly recorded in the way that a parent watches a child grow, but we are all very important, part of a finely tuned web and each part is registered, the spider knows, the spider has spun the web, the spider knows each break, each section, each strand'

'A telescope on the battlements of a castle, steel rivets, metal, it could be guns, gun emplacement. I'm looking at the stars, they're very brilliant, there's no other light'

'looking at reflections in the window, families; a sense of Hogmanay'

'Somebody's saying old power... accordion music'

'this ancient dragon, old power... family feuds... sense the old power... Looking up at the stars, this clarity, the brilliance of stars, the telescope seeing far, the whole universe out there, never ending. It's this sense of in the stars are hidden patterns, hidden information, there's hope in the seeds of new life, nothing's stuck, the old shapes will be shaken and this new brilliance and wisdom will come through and all the old quarrels will be forgotten... That's all'

15/12/2015

Freddie is trying to get through'

'Kazakhstan and the space ship... That's a connection with Freddie, he said the astronaut was going to play one of the songs to calm him before take-off, it was going to be a Queen song, he said thankyou Freddie, that was in the news...'

'a wonderful thing that someone who's died has left something precious, something that can inspire other people, that the works of their hands and minds endures, it outlives the flesh. That is moving, it makes me want to cry, it's beautiful. I left a legacy, Freddie...'

'That's very poignant to blast off into space with the words of a Queen song….. the question, … is this reality? That was being questioned… what is reality? That was the song he chose……that to turn fiction into reality, whatever you imagine can mould the physical reality'

'People were laughed at for assuming they could fly and that man could fly to the stars'

'It's like the words… We are such stuff that dreams are made on and our little lives are rounded in sleep… Maybe that's the crux of it, we have to question what is real, we have to doubt our own version of reality'

'And they have all the flags on the space station, you have to notice they are all made up of primary colours, permutation, that notion of individual nation, variations on a theme but flags turn to tatters, they're changing colours all the time and so it all goes wrong, to put a flag on the moon is to lay claim on what is universal that's why it all went wrong. When the centre is at every point everyone is everyone, there's no individuality, it's illusion'

' see this great sun like a ball of individuals but they're all connected like the rays of the sun, all smiling and laughing, all the astronauts and those around each other they all have their roots in the sun like the petals of a sun flower, it's a big smile…'

'floating through space like a featherweight… seeing fireworks like a festival… fun… life is fun…'

'End on that note of a funfair or a fanfare… funfair or fanfare, that's all connected with Freddie… Thank you Freddie…'

Printed in Great Britain
by Amazon